www.InThreeEasySteps.com

how *you* can
KILL AL QAEDA
(in 3 easy steps)

HOWARD CLARK

Light of New Orleans Publishing

Manufactured in the United States of America

The views expressed in this publication are the author's and do not imply endorsement by the Office of Intelligence and Analysis, Department of Homeland Security or any other U.S. Government agency. He is writing this book as an independent citizen. Nothing in this book represents the views, findings, or conclusions of the U.S. or any other government or government-affiliated organization. In fact, any government information operations would lose credibility because most Muslim communities abroad distrust the U.S. Government.

Library of Congress Cataloging-in-Publication Data
Clark, Howard, 1978 -
How you can kill Al Qaeda : in 3 easy steps / Howard clark.
p. cm.
Includes bibliographical references.
ISBN 978-0-9714076-5-7 (pbk. : alk. paper)
1. Qaida (Organization) 2. Terrorism. I. Title.
HV6432.5.Q2H66 2009
363.325'16--dc22

2008050683

Dedicated to

Captain John W. Maloney,
United States Marine Corps,
killed in Iraq, June 16, 2005.
Hero.

All of the author's profits from this book will be sent to Afghan Health & Development Services (www.ahds.org).

While al-Qaeda and the Taliban intimidate and kill Muslims in Afghanistan, the Afghan Health & Development Services helps to rehabilitate their country's health infrastructure. Founded by Afghans, this non-profit, non-governmental, and non-political organization trains medical staff and provides comprehensive primary health care services to those in need.

contents

how *you* can KILL AL QAEDA

(in 3 easy steps)

introduction

I cannot believe that I have to write this book. I cannot believe that it has come down to this. Since 2001, the U.S. has spent half of a trillion dollars in an attempt to defeat al-Qaeda to no avail. So, in this little book, I will give you—*you* being any reader or private organization—the three easy steps to kill al-Qaeda.

Nothing in this book will shock a seasoned Arabist or student of Islam—those the government has ignored and left out of important planning meetings for too long. It doesn't take Einstein to unravel al-Qaeda quickly. It takes a dose of common sense and some awareness that Islam is *not* a dangerous religion and al-Qaeda lives and grows off its ability to persuade some Muslims to follow its violent ideals.

The enemy is not conservative or constructionist Islam. The enemy are not devoted Muslims or Islamist groups, such as the Egyptian Muslim Brotherhood, striving for freedom. Conservative and strict interpretations of Islam are not gateway drugs to violent extremism. Despite what some journalists think, al-Qaeda adherents are very often not drawn from conservative schools or communities. In fact devoted religious leaders are often the best answer to keeping young potential extremists peaceful.

This book is not some ivory tower academic theory or impractical government assessment outsourced to the brightest contractors, with ideas that soar five miles above the ground, resembling mental masturbation more than usable wisdom. Instead this is a practical guide to end the "war on terrorism." It will drive all those that profit from this "war"—from contracted analysts to contracted security forces to weapons contractors—nuts. They will deride this book while they continue to sell this "war" as a long "war" to ensure their continued profit.

This book also does not give directions to stop individual terrorist attacks—something the brave women and men of the United States armed forces and law enforcement do successfully everyday. Instead, I am interested only in strategic and *permanent* defeat of al-Qaeda.

The simple elimination of individual extremists in defense of the Homeland and U.S. interests can be likened to the Greek monster Hydra—for every one head severed, the monster would re-grow two more. This even goes for Usama Bin Ladin. Even if (or when) Bin Ladin is offed, his deputies are ready and itching to take over—perhaps with a more violent strategy. And of course his death would be seen as a martyrdom and powerful symbol for decades to come.

In order to destroy al-Qaeda's brand of mass murder in the name of religion, we must cut off their main strength: *popular support*. An effort must be made to drive an irreparable wedge between Islamic terrorists and nonviolent Muslims, so that recruitment pools and support dry up. Then, al-Qaeda will wither and die.

Before I write anything further, I need to nail some definitions down. First off, there is no such thing as a "war on terrorism." Terrorism is a tactic. Waging a war on terrorism would be like waging a war on infantry frontal assaults. It's absurd.

I also must define the enemy. Instead of paying contractors to write 50 volumes on who the enemy is exactly (An idea? Particular people? Transnational movement?), I would suggest simply that we are fighting al-Qaeda. I will define al-Qaeda as those regenerative, elusive leaders probably living in western Pakistan who promote a worldwide militant threat against the West and inspire individuals and groups to conduct violence in the name of religion.

By the way, al-Qaeda means "the base" and is properly transliterated as "al-Qa'ida" (pronounced al-KAH-ee-da), but it is popularly spelled "al-Qaeda" in the United States and Great Britain.

So, without further ado, allow me to tell you how to kill them.

In Brief...

the bottom line upfront

Problem:

Al-Qaeda is, at this very moment, the greatest threat to U.S. national security. Al-Qaeda leadership effectively inspires Muslims to kill U.S. citizens. Through its unchallenged online messaging to the Muslim public, al-Qaeda garners its critical support and future recruits. Although there is a plethora of influential counter-al-Qaeda ideologues, these counter-voices lack the online marketing to reach general Muslim audiences, and so are unable to undermine al-Qaeda's violent messages.

Solution:

Undermine al-Qaeda messaging to completely isolate al-Qaeda from Muslim communities worldwide.

THE THREE STEPS:

I. Identify
II. Translate
III. Disseminate

Identify, **Translate**, and **Disseminate** online persuasive and independent counter-al-Qaeda messages on the Internet —*the* primary media on which al-Qaeda markets their messages. No collaboration with or permission from these counter-voices is necessary.

Who can do this?

Any individual (Muslim, Christian, Jewish, or any religion), group of volunteers, non-profit company, publishing house, or organization anywhere in the world that is independent of government influence.

As for the individual, let's face it, most people are busy enough as it is. That's why I've made is so that a person by themselves need only pick and choose what they want to take from this already short book. They can then disseminate the proper messages in about half an hour total. I'll show you how.

Target Audience:

Mainstream Muslim communities, which al-Qaeda depends on for support and future recruits. Most of those already headed down the path of violence in the name of religion may be too far gone for rehabilitation. Rather than trying to de-radicalize full blown terrorists, we will focus on preventing the radicalization of mainstream Muslims.

Why is someone else not already doing this?

There is currently no effective counter-messaging campaign against al-Qaeda, primarily because governments focus on stopping specific attacks versus strategically destroying the root threat: *al-Qaeda's ability to persuade mainstream Muslims*. Success of police and military operations which arrest and kill al-Qaeda operators and supporters is measurable and allows government leaders to enjoy small and strategically meaningless victories, while al-Qaeda messaging generates new operators and supporters.

endstate

Drive an irreparable wedge between al-Qaeda and Muslim communities worldwide on which al-Qaeda depends for recruits, financing, supplies, moral support, and legitimacy.

More specifically:

- *Sow seeds of doubt among al-Qaeda affiliates and supporters.*

- *Solidify beliefs of those already against al-Qaeda.*

- *Deter those on the fence ideologically.*

- *Waste al-Qaeda's time. Keep them on the ideological defensive. Keep al-Qaeda leaders and pro-al-Qaeda authors, theorists, and supporters consumed with responding to criticism instead of attempting to widen their support further.*

target audience

Wider societal support is al-Qaeda's lifeblood. Even at the most visceral level, Muslim suicide attackers rely on some semblance of public approval to be willing to make the ultimate sacrifice. Suicide bombers seek death specifically because at least part of Muslim societies venerates the sacrifice. Without wide acceptance—if terrorists are ineligible for martyrdom status in any of the world's Muslim communities—recruits will less likely be willing to die in the name of God.

Those susceptible to radicalization could be anywhere. Violent extremists share no common profile. They are poor and rich, young and old, and reflect the diversity of the world's Muslim communities. This includes those that join terrorist groups as well as those who support them either aggressively or passively by turning a blind eye. Any counter ideology marketing campaign must therefore target every Muslim or person thinking of conversion.

Often, journalists sell the idea that somehow terrorists are poor, desperate, and ignorant. However, there is overwhelming evidence to suggest no such correlation:

- A 2006 Gallup World Poll of over 9,000 interviews in nine predominantly-Muslim countries found that radical Muslims are more likely to be wealthy and to have stayed in school longer than moderates.

- In a 2004 study of 132 terrorists, over 60% had some college education and 4% had a doctoral degree, making this sample pool more educated than most in the third world.

- A 2006 study of 242 European violent extremists concluded that socioeconomic background and criminal history of terrorists are similar to backgrounds of most young persons in immigrant Muslim communities in Europe.

- In a sample of 232 Arab suicide attackers associated with Lebanese and Palestinian groups and al-Qaeda from 1980-2003, a study found that suicide bombers had similar education levels and socioeconomic status to the Lebanese and Palestinian publics.

- Recent interviews with Palestinian suicide bomber dispatchers and failed suicide attackers concluded that many terrorists did not have financial difficulties. Failed attackers held a standard of living comparable with most Palestinians.

- Recent evidence also supports the dissociation of extremism and wealth: the failed June 2007 U.K. airport attackers were well-educated. All suspects were medical doctors but one who was an engineer with a PhD.

The bottom line is that any counter-ideology campaign must target Muslims as widely as possible in as many languages as possible. Anecdotal evidence suggests that some mainstream Muslims could even turn to violence while seeking an education in a place with opportunity, freedom, political expression, and wealth. Modern extremism's "godfather" Sayyid Qutb's education exchange in the United States led him to despise what he perceived as the West's immorality. His observations while a student in the United States sparked his journey into radicalism after he returned home to Egypt.

Sayyid Qutb in prison, before his execution
by the Egyptian government in 1966

problem

Al-Qaeda is winning the war of ideas. Facts and pictures illustrate al-Qaeda's narrative of Islam under attack from the West. Images of Guantanamo and Abu Ghraib display the United States humiliating Muslims and help to provide al-Qaeda with new recruitment pools and public support.

Al-Qaeda's message has helped to alarm Muslims abroad over U.S. intentions. A majority of Muslims view the United States as a potential threat. Today, majorities in Bangladesh (93%), Morocco (92%), Indonesia (85%), Malaysia (81%), Turkey (77%), Palestinian Territory (73%), Pakistan (73%), Jordan (67%), Egypt (65%), Lebanon (64%), and Kuwait (63%) are "very" or "somewhat" worried that the United States could become a military threat. The Muslim world distrusts the U.S. government.

Violence in the name of Islam has even become a fad in some Muslim countries. "Jihadi cool," distrust of the United States, and hatred for U.S. "humiliation" of Muslims have permeated Muslim communities worldwide. Al-Qaeda has helped to unify parts of the Muslim world against the United States.

Al-Qaeda has stayed on message from its inception. From the beginning, al-Qaeda has warned Muslims of the "U.S. threat." As the U.S. government continues its missions in the Middle East—no matter how vital for international security and important for the protection of Muslims—the United States plays out al-Qaeda's message. Bin Ladin and his chief deputy Ayman al-Zawahiri (pronounced EYE-man az-zah-WA-her-ree) published their narrative clearly in 1998 and continue to stay on message condemning U.S. policies:

1) On U.S. military presence in the Middle East, Bin Ladin and Zawahiri wrote:

> *First, for over seven years the United States has been occupying the lands of Islam in the holiest of places, the Arabian Peninsula, plundering its riches, dictating to it rulers, humiliating its people, terrorizing its neighbors, and turning its bases in the Peninsula into a spearhead through which to fight the neighboring Muslim peoples. If some people have in the past argued about the fact of the occupation, all the people of the Peninsula have now acknowledged it. The*

best proof of this is the Americans' continuing aggression against the Iraqi people using the Peninsula as a staging post, even though all its rulers are against their territories being used to that end, but they are helpless.

2) 1990s U.S. containment policies of Iraq:

Second, despite the great devastation inflicted on the Iraqi people by the crusader-Zionist alliance, and despite the huge number of those killed, which has exceeded one million... despite all this, the Americans are once again trying to repeat the horrific massacres, as though they are not content with the protracted blockade imposed after the ferocious war or the fragmentation and devastation. So here they come to annihilate what is left of this people and to humiliate their Muslim neighbors.

3) U.S. support for Israel:

Third, if the Americans' aims in these wars are religious and economic, the aim is also to serve the Jews' petty state and divert attention from its occupation of Jerusalem and murder of Muslims there. The best proof of this is their eagerness to destroy Iraq, the strongest neighboring Arab state, and their endeavor to fragment all the states of the region such as Iraq, Saudi Arabia, Egypt, and Sudan into paper statelets and through their disunion and weakness to guarantee Israel's survival and the continuation of the brutal crusade occupation of the Peninsula.

Today, record numbers of U.S. troops in the Middle East, combat operations in Iraq, and support for Israel continue to provide evidence to support al-Qaeda's story of Islam under attack from the West.

Even well intentioned U.S. operations in Muslim countries fail to assuage Muslim fears. No amount of tsunami aid, earthquake aid, humanitarian missions, Iraqi despots deposed, or Muslims protected (operations in Kuwait, Saudi Arabia, Bosnia, and Kosovo to name a few) appears to temper foreign Muslim anger. These activities actually play directly into the hands of militants who blame inequities on the unwanted foreign presence.

On the same token, messages from the U.S. government fall onto deaf or resentful ears. Any U.S. Department of State public diplomacy statement or U.S. military counter-violence statement is lost on most Muslims abroad. The United States does not have the credentials in Muslim communities to persuade. Distrust is too deep. Furthermore, Muslim anti-violence ideologues would lose complete credibility, influence, and livelihood through open or rumored collaboration with U.S. representatives. *Counter messages must, therefore, come from sources popularly considered independent of governments*: only amplified voices of legitimate independent sources can be effective.

Currently, the Internet is *the* primary media on which al-Qaeda markets their messages. Al-Qaeda does not use physical literature (books and pamphlets) to garner support because Middle Eastern, Northern African, Southern Asian, and some European governments arrest Muslims in possession of extremist or al-Qaeda-supporting literature.

Currently, al-Qaeda's robust, reinforced, and redundant network of easily accessible online narratives and films in multiple languages and on numerous media platforms is unchallenged. Al-Qaeda pours money, time, and manpower into their online empire. Some analysts suggest that other factors—such as friendships with extremists and charismatic radical preachers—contribute more to radicalization than messaging. But al-Qaeda's growing focus on messaging suggests its centrality to gaining recruits and supporters. Many factors play a part to radicalization, but messaging is the vital vein.

Al-Qaeda messages on thousands of websites command Muslims to kill or support the killing of U.S. citizens to defend Islam against the United States. Specifically, al-Qaeda centers its messages on U.S. support for Israel, U.S. troops in Iraq and Afghanistan, and past prisoner mistreatment in Guantanamo Bay and Abu Ghraib to garner anger against the United States and persuade Muslims that the United States government and citizens repress and humiliate Muslims.

Al-Qaeda's Media Empire

This messaging radicalizes Muslims. A publicized U.K. study, based on information from hundreds of incarcerated terrorists and terrorist associates, concludes that effective online messaging is crucial to radicalization. A Homeland Security Policy Institute study of eight major terrorism cases—to include the 2004 Madrid bombers and 2005 London bombers—concludes that online messaging was critical to radicalization. Internet messages directly radicalized the convicted planners of the 2007 Fort Dix New Jersey plot to kill U.S. soldiers, according to court documents. The terrorists had planned to storm the base and murder U.S. soldiers and civilians with small arms fire.

Meanwhile, counter al-Qaeda voices are not translated and not available on the Internet.

Typically, a Muslim wishing to learn about one of the primary grievances against the United States (Israel, Iraq, Afghanistan, Guantanamo Bay, and Abu Ghraib) will do an internet search on these subjects and find al-Qaeda messages using these perceived injustices to justify violence in the name of religion.

For example, on October 17, 2008, if you Googled "U.S., support, Israel, Jihad, religion," the fifth hit was a website supporting violence: themodernreligion.com/jihad.html (even when doing a search in the U.S. and in English). On the same day, if you Googled "Iraq, United States, Jihad," sites with links to extremist messages popped up such as jihadunspun.com. These sites, with religious and moralistic answers, are the ones that curious and/or angry Muslims will click on. They overtly present religious and ideological reasons to justify violence. There are also portals through legitimate sites that will steer any curious user to radical propaganda. And trying these same searches in Arabic yields far worse results.

Just one of many examples of professional, easily searchable, radicalizing message streams is the "Jihad Press." Found in English and Arabic online searches, the professional-looking and extremely well-written Arabic online newspaper advocates al-Qaeda violence as an answer to everyday Muslim concerns over Western imposition in the Islamic World.

From his new home in Yemen, New Mexico-born Anwar Nassar al-Awlaki publishes written and audio lectures commanding Muslims all over the world to attack the United States and its interests at all times under any and all circumstances. His lecture "Constants on the Path of Jihad," for example, persuades Muslims towards violence in no uncertain terms and is available widely on the internet. In simple, straight-forward American vernacular, the lecture is available on hundreds of independent websites. His lecture is also littered all over youtube.com.

Anwar al-Awlaki also posted "44 Ways of Supporting Jihad" on January 5, 2009, on his website. The essay commands every Muslim to focus every resource and effort towards violence against Western and secular governments and details how Muslims can help al-Qaeda marketing. Awlaki explains to readers how to identify, translate, and disseminate violent teachings and commands in support of al-Qaeda. Within only 24 hours, this essay received over 1,000 downloads, and 61 other websites had already reposted the paper.

Another example of an extremist website easily found online was inshallahshahedd.muslimpar.com in October 2007. This site, run by an American Muslim in North Carolina, offered up translations and sound bites of messages encouraging violent attacks against Americans. The U.S. Military Academy's Combating Terrorism Center actually assessed this site to be in the top 100 of the most active English-language radical sites. And it certainly did not help that the *New York Times* published a story about the site in October 2007 skyrocketing viewership and searchability. This site alone had links to dozens of other violence-advocating sites in English such as theunjustmedia.com, truthline.wordpress.com, and amreekan.wordpress.com. These examples only offer a smattering of what can be found online that pushes al-Qaeda messages of violence to the masses.

Messages that persuasively argue that killing is against religion do not appear during these online searches and therefore cannot undermine or even compete with al-Qaeda messaging. Even if a website sparked a kernel of doubt against al-Qaeda's ideas, this would be infinitely more than the current situation.

solution

Identify, **Translate**, and **Disseminate** persuasive and independent counter-al-Qaeda messages onto a robust network of easily searchable websites in numerous languages. These websites should dominate online search results over al-Qaeda websites.

I. Identify

Authors of persuasive counter-al-Qaeda messages are popularly considered independent of governments, especially Arab secular, E.U., and U.S. governments. Their arguments use reason, emotion, and religious grounding to undermine al-Qaeda and al-Qaeda-affiliate justifications for violence.

Counter-al-Qaeda writers, to be effective, will normally be anti-United States, anti-Israel, anti-West, and even anti-democracy. Such views are necessary evils and often the only way for speakers and writers to claim independence from the West and Western allies to maintain credibility.

Arguments will not contest al-Qaeda's claim of the need to defend Islam against the West. Instead they will focus on the heresy and practical limitations of al-Qaeda violence. These messages are found in local, national, and international newspapers; online media sources; published books; references and quotes in popular English academic and policy journals; and independent websites. I will provide examples later.

II. Translate

Just as al-Qaeda and al-Qaeda-affiliate marketers translate their radical literature and speeches into other languages quickly and accurately, someone must accurately translate counter-al-Qaeda messages.

The importance of translation is highlighted in the radicalization of Mohammad Sidique Khan, mastermind of the July 7, 2005, attacks on London's subway. According to his brother, Khan could not relate to the local non-violent imam because of the language barrier. Khan spoke English. The imam taught only in Urdu and Arabic.

In the future, people like Khan should have access to counter-al-Qaeda ideas in clear English (or in his or her native tongue). Translations must include African, European, and Southeast and Southwest Asian languages: Modern Standard Arabic, Spanish, French, German, Farsi, Bahasa Indonesia, Urdu, Turkish, Pashto, Chinese, Kurdish, Hindi, Somali, Malay, Tamil, Tagalog, Thai, Chechen, Serbo-Croat, and Dutch for starters. Reputable companies throughout the world can fully and properly translate statements and texts for the right price. For example, Language One will translate a page of text into all of the twenty aforementioned languages for about $1720.

III. Disseminate

Websites with counter-al-Qaeda messages should litter the internet with sound bites, powerful quotes, pictures, and promotion of sources' credentials and independence.

Sites must use anonymous host servers (plenty in the United States, Canada, and Europe—the same that al-Qaeda uses). Sites must be designed for search engine optimization to ensure they appear first during searches. Sites must be searchable by the key words which al-Qaeda uses to gain support: *Israel, Palestine, Iraq, Afghanistan, Guantanamo Bay, Abu Ghraib,* and *U.S. military bases in Saudi Arabia.*

Sites must be linked to popular Islamist websites and blogs—it's easy to enter URLs on blogs. At the very least, Muslims susceptible to radicalization should have easy internet access to a plethora of sources that compete with al-Qaeda's justifications of violence.

7 types of messages to Identify, Translate, and Disseminate

You may choose one or any number of the following to be effective.

1) Messages from Former Violent Extremists

Those who used to execute or promote violence in the name of religion—who now appear to modify their views on violence—often wield the required respect and independence from government influence to persuade Muslims to condemn radicalism.

Reformed terrorist leader and ideologue Sayyid Imam's 2007 Arabic reversal played well in Arabic news sources, but the book has not been translated, quoted, and widely disseminated (he wrote the text in his prison cell in Egypt where he has been since 2004). His renunciation of al-Qaeda's terrorist tactics confronts killing over ethnicity, use of human shields, and destruction of non-Muslim property.

In the words of Sayyid Imam:

"There is nothing that invokes the anger of God and His wrath like the unwarranted spilling of blood and wrecking property."

"There is no such thing in Islam as ends justifying the means."

"If vice becomes mixed with virtue, all becomes sinful."

"Oh, you young people, do not be deceived by the heroes of the internet, the leaders of the microphones, who are launching statements inciting youth while living in a distant cave... they have thrown many others before you into the infernos, graves, and prisons."

"Those who have triggered clashes and pressed their brothers into unequal military confrontations are specialists neither in fatwas nor in military affairs."

"On the day of judgment every double crosser will have a banner up his anus proportional to his treachery."

In addition to his persuasive reasoning Sayyid Imam has "street cred"—he's been on the front line of violent Islamist movements and was formerly at the ideological helm of al-Qaeda. He was even mentor to Usama Bin Ladin and his deputy Zawahiri. West Point's Combating Terrorism Center assesses that ideologically *Sayyid Imam is as influential as Usama bin Ladin*. His pre-prison, pre-reformed, violent texts still influence al-Qaeda leadership. His *Foundations of the Preparation for Jihad* is the book al-Qaeda uses to justify violent actions and establish its group structure worldwide. His influence could give the renunciation maximum impact.

Sayyid Imam's critics claim that the Egyptian government tortured and forced the recantation. His detractors even maintain that Sayyid Imam is a pawn of the West. Nonetheless, continued worldwide reverence for Sayyid Imam will likely even outweigh al-Qaeda criticism. Zawahiri wrote a 188-page defense against Imam's book, which

1) Gave Sayyid Imam further legitimacy and publicity.
2) Squandered al-Qaeda leadership time.
3) Revealed al-Qaeda's fear of the effect of counter-violence messages.
4) Forced Zawahiri to restate his justifications for violent attacks that inevitably kill civilians.

Other reformed extremist messages also have the potential to undermine al-Qaeda's ideology, such as bin Ladin's former mentor Salman al-Awdah's 2007 editorial attack on bin Ladin; Gamaah Islamiyah's (a former Egyptian terrorist group) 1990s recantations; former terrorist leader of Southeast Asia Jamaah Islamiyah Nasir Abas' interviews and book *Exposing Jamaah Islamiyah,* criticizing al-Qaeda-style violence; and rehabilitated, imprisoned Saudi extremist renunciations. You can learn the location of these texts and find some in full at InThreeEasySteps.com.

These authors provide novel arguments that challenge al-Qaeda's tired reuse of theories that date back decades. These new voices point out al-Qaeda's strategic failure to defeat the West and govern, their willingness to wantonly kill Muslims, and religious misunderstandings. Al-Qaeda continues to invent new hooks in an attempt to persuade new audiences—such as Zawahiri's 2007 statement feigning empathy with African-American discrimination in the United States—but their base message of violence to defend Islam against Western aggressors remains the same. *Former-extremist messages have the potential to break this pattern—the potential to be fresh and newsworthy.*

2) Fatwas (Religious Commands) against Terrorism

Some religious edicts from independent sources have the ability to persuade Muslims worldwide. One example is the potentially tide-shifting February 2008 Deobandi fatwa of

6,000 members in India against violence in the name of religion, publicly reconfirmed by the members in October 2008. The conservative Muslim Deobandi-sect leadership and ideals have influenced the Taliban, and the Deobandi ideologues appear independent from government influence. And as with all statements, actual government collusion is irrelevant—only the appearance of independence is necessary to lend statements credibility. This text can be found at InThreeEasySteps.com.

Fatwas that paint al-Qaeda as the widely villainized heretical Islamist group the *Khawarij* (also known as *Kharijites*—pronounced KAR-i-jites) can be especially effective. The term can generate visceral repulsion due to the group's infamous reputation in Islamic history (in reality some sects were non-violent and in fact continue to survive today). When the term is used today, it normally refers to the most violent of the *Kharijite* sect—puritanical extremists who killed Islam's fourth leader (or "Caliph"). The word *Kharijite* has become a harsh insult. The group is today popularly considered the heretical, perverted enemies in Islamic history. Several governments including Saudi Arabia and Indonesia have used the term to describe terrorists publicly, and al-Qaeda has spent time and money to defend against the accusation. And these defensive efforts reveal the power of the insult.

The most violent sect of the *Kharijites* built an independent community in which they claimed to follow the Qur'an (the exact word of God as told to the Prophet Muhammad) and *Sunna* (record of the Prophet's actions) strictly and literally. From this base, they waged violent attacks in the name of Allah. They saw the world in black and white: either you were a devout Muslim who abided by the *Kharijites'* particular version of Islam, or you were an enemy of Allah. Muslims who did not buy into their militant Islam were condemned to death. For *Kharijites*, the ends justified the means. Violence was not just allowed, it was compulsory. Many Muslim scholars consider the *Kharijites* ignorant of Islam and too quick to judge people as infidels.

Today, al-Qaeda and its supporters also justify violence against non-Muslims and Muslims who do not adhere to their particular style of Islam. This ideology resembles the *Kharijites*. As one of al-Qaeda's forefathers, Muhammad al-Faraj, wrote in his influential book *The Neglected Duty*: "There is no doubt that the idols of this world can only disappear through the power of the sword."

Suicide, murder, mutilation, or anything else is permissible to attain a sprawling Islamic Empire ruled under strict Islamic law as defined by the peculiar views of al-Qaeda much like the *Kharijites*. Condemning al-Qaeda to the *Kharijite* fringe explains to Muslim communities that terrorists will be condemned to hell.

The argument that modern *Kharijites* do not follow the way of the Prophet and are therefore doomed for eternity can be an effective counter-voice to al-Qaeda propaganda.

Likewise, comparing al-Qaeda to the *Qaramita*—a fanatical 9th and 10th century movement that killed thousands of Muslims in the name of God—will also damage al-Qaeda's reputation. In a September 2007 statement, top al-Qaeda lieutenant Abu Yahya al-Libi even admitted that comparisons to the *Qaramita* would injure al-Qaeda credibility in the eyes of mainstream Muslims.

3) MESSAGES THAT STRESS AL-QAEDA'S HERESY

Exposing al-Qaeda and their supporters' hypocritical devotion to radical thinkers will reveal their heresy. Despite al-Qaeda leaders' claims that they adhere only to the original texts of Islam, al-Qaeda deifies a cadre of ideologues. Such reverence to inspirational intellectuals—or *any* human being for that matter—is *sacrilege* to devout Muslims. And their regard for these ideologues' ideas while alleging to reject generations of scholarly interpretation of Islam's primary manuscripts is hypocrisy.

Violent radical authors, by interpreting Islam and how Muslims must act, execute a form of forbidden innovation (known as *bid'a*). They essentially follow *tawassuf*—the practice of revering religious figures acting as intercessors with God. The Prophet Muhammad said, "I am leaving you two things and you will never go astray as long as you cling to them. They are the Book of Allah and my Sunna." Therefore, al-Qaeda, who follow books *other* than those Muhammad clearly promoted, are *heretics*—incapable of representing or fighting for Muslims.

Al-Qaeda leadership and supporters sell themselves as devoted *Salafis*—those who venerate the first generations of Islam and reject Islamic scholarship, innovation, and interpretations of the Qur'an and Sunna. Most Salafis seek peaceful religious purity or political action, but al-Qaeda betrays this faith with their devotion to violent interpretations of the Qur'an and perverted innovations to justify attacks.

For example, Ibn Taymiyyah (pronounced ibn tie-MEE-ya, a 14th century writer) is still the most influential extremist writer today. Ibn Taymiyyah justified violence against foreigners. His message still resounds with Al-Qaeda and affiliates worldwide, and he is commonly quoted in al-Qaeda and affiliate messages.

Of the modern authors, Sayyid Qutb has the greatest influence. His commentary on the Qur'an, along with his seminal book *Milestones*, continues to inspire extremists to act violently. Zawahiri has openly followed and quoted from Qutb's texts.

Usama Bin Ladin, himself, is one of the top thirteen most influential modern militant authors. As the popular icon for a violent united worldwide front, he influences radicals worldwide and simultaneously contradicts his claim to be a devoted Muslim dedicated to true Islam.

Dubbing al-Qaeda followers as "binladinists," "qutbists," "farajists," and "taymiyyahists"—because they openly praise these ideologues such as Sayyid Qutb, Muhammad al-Faraj, and Ibn Taymiyyah—helps to reveal al-Qaeda's blatant hypocrisy. Extremists are talking out of both sides of their mouths—touting strict following of the Qur'an and Sunna and nothing else, yet also heretically praising and promoting human beings.

Messages from any Muslim appearing independent of government influence on al-Qaeda's heresy will dissuade mainstream Muslims from supporting the group.

4) MESSAGES FOCUSING ON INNOCENT VICTIMS

Arguments that killing innocents is core to the al-Qaeda mission will sway Muslims worldwide. Messages accompanied by descriptions and images of elderly, child, and handicapped victims will be especially effective.

There is already evidence that innocent victims turn Muslims off to al-Qaeda. Wide counter-violence messaging would deepen the effect. Muslims in Africa and Asia have increasingly rejected suicide bombings and violence against civilians from 2002 to 2007. The downward trend indicates that advocates of suicide attacks are capable of changing their views on a substantial scale in a short time. Statements emphasizing civilian casualties of terrorist attacks would likely encourage further rejection of terrorist tactics.

The extensive Pew Study found support for terrorist tactics has declined in seven out of eight countries for which the survey had data since 2002:

Lebanon:	74% → 34%
Bangladesh:	44% → 20%
Pakistan:	33% → 9%
Jordan:	43% → 23%
Indonesia:	26% → 10%
Tanzania:	18% → 11%
Nigeria:	47% → 42%
Turkey:	12% → 16%

The study provides a road map to tear apart the radical ideology that it is okay to kill even innocents in the name of Allah. Muslims, by a wide margin, do not approve of the tactic, and translated and disseminated messages should further solidify al-Qaeda's critics and avert new recruits and supporters.

Just as al-Qaeda uses symbols of Muslim humiliation—Gitmo and Abu Ghraib, for example—the counter messages should employ images of civilian casualties.

Extremist propaganda presents graphic pictures of Muslim victims of Western attacks to garner support. Popular newspapers in North Africa and the Middle East also publish graphic photographs of these attack victims. Similarly, graphic images of terrorist victims—to include women and children—may help further erode support for terrorist tactics. These images must go beyond front page *New York Times* pictures of suicide attack victims in Iraq. They must go beyond London-based Arabic newspaper *Al-Qud*'s black and white photographs of beheaded Iraqis. *The images must be burned into the memories of every viewer.*

Effective photos do not necessarily have to be bloodier or gorier than al-Qaeda's images of victims of Western attacks. American film critics widely consider that the most disturbing images from movies are not necessarily gory. The winter breath leaving a murdered Jewish architect in *Schindler's List* and an off-camera ear slicing in *Reservoir Dogs* unsettled moviegoers far more than any second-rate, gory, B-movie ultraviolence.

Likewise, some of the most influential American photography was not necessarily explicit. National Geographic's photo of a green-eyed Afghan girl sparked more reader reaction than any bloody shots from Russia's war in Afghanistan in the 1980s. A picture of a crying Vietnamese child impacted support for the U.S. war in Vietnam more than any battle images.

Images of terrorist victims can be found on the internet:

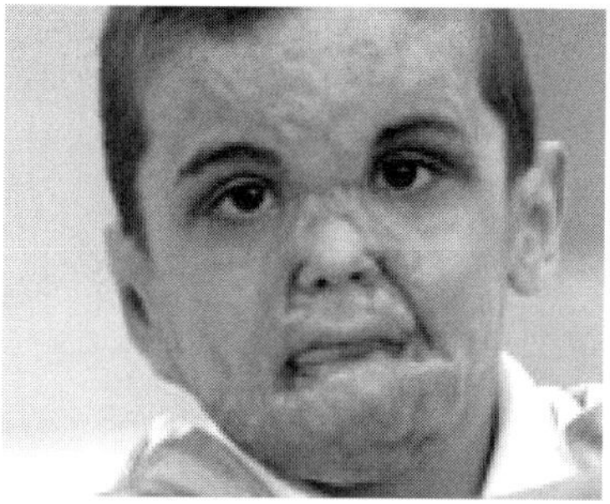

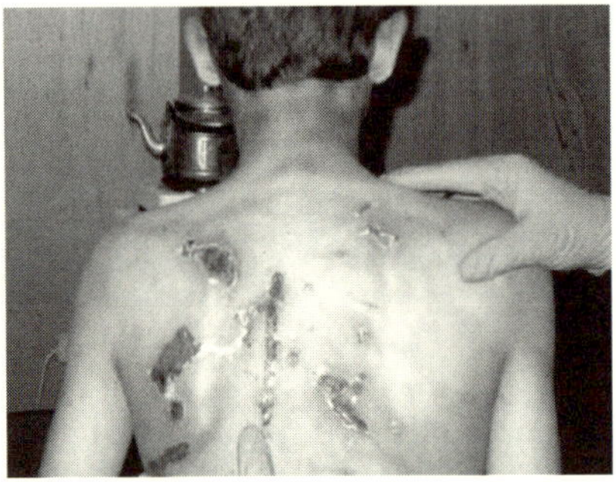

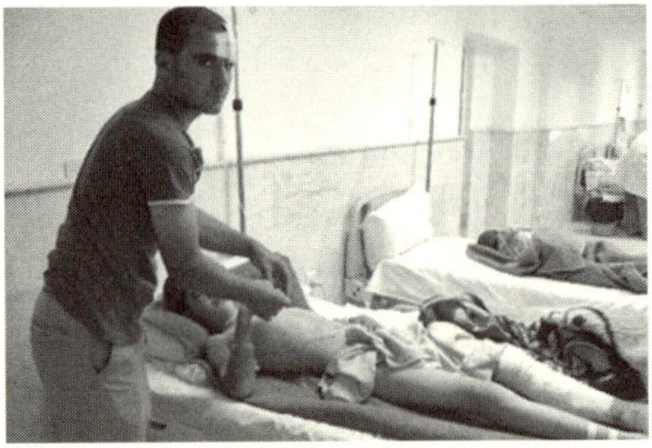

You can find these and other images in color, and their credited sources, on InThreeEasySteps.com.

5) Messages Stressing the Inevitability of Failure

Few Muslims want to support a lost cause. So one stream of anti-al-Qaeda messaging should explain that al-Qaeda efforts are in vain and ultimately selfishly arrogant—stressing in reasoned and practical terms the *impossibility of success through violence*.

Messages should erase completely any apparent connection between current terrorist tactics and future success, no matter how many generations al-Qaeda says they plan to attack the West. Messages must show that U.S. security, law enforcement, civilian vigilance, and national confidence are too great.

Al-Qaeda has consistently justified attacks as the only opportunity for success and has written extensively on the necessity and obligation of violence in reaction to criticism that their cause is lost and therefore self-serving and unholy. Such reactions from al-Qaeda underline the potential success of counter-messaging that al-Qaeda's tactics are destined to fail.

Al-Qaeda's narrative stresses that the movement will continue long after the leaders' deaths. Bin Ladin and all his deputies are openly aware of their mortality. And fighters have gladly died with the knowledge that success would be certain—even if it takes generations. Foreign and Iraqi fighters willingly remained in Fallujah, Iraq in November 2004 knowing they would die as Marines surrounded and entered the town. Insurgents near al-Qa'im, on the border with Syria, holed up in the basements of houses to die fighting Americans in July 2005. They believed that they were one piece of a greater fight that would last perhaps centuries before victory. Take any possibility of future victory away, and new recruits will have great doubts about dying for a dying cause.

The message, however, must focus only on the connection between tactics and goal. The identified messages should not judge the goal itself to be unattainable—the goal being the West out of the Middle East and reestablishment of the old Islamic Empire spanning southwest Asia to Spain.

Thus far, continued counter-terrorism military and police policies do not appear to substantially stop future terrorist attacks or drain the morale of terrorists. The attacks just keep coming. Messages must, therefore, aggressively drill the fact into the minds of Muslims that failure is inevitable: a hundred or a thousand generations of violence in the name of God against the United States will not bring a restored Islamic Empire. Proof is that they have not come close to hurting or destroying the fabric of the United States.

6) Messages That Circulate Stories of Infiltration of Al-Qaeda's Top Websites

Shutting down al-Qaeda affiliate and supporting websites (which independent groups and individuals attempt to do daily) does nothing. The sites pop up sometimes minutes after shutdown. Instead messages should attack the *integrity of site hosts* to undermine confidence in the independence and veracity of al-Qaeda's sites.

Al-Qaeda relies on the image of integrity at the top echelon of its marketing pyramid: "Al-Sahab," "Al-Fajr," and the "Global Islamic Media Front" marketing networks. For example, if you spread the knowledge that the Indonesian government has infiltrated "Al-Fajr Network" websites, this can greatly decrease user confidence.

Global Islamic Media Front

A recent media rumor of Saudi government infiltration shut down and ratcheted up security for the entire Global Islamic Media Front (hundreds of websites) temporarily. This cost al-Qaeda time, money, and a nosedive in user confidence in the host's integrity.

Such stories can be found in local or international online newspapers. But as of yet, these stories are not translated and widely disseminated.

7) Stories of Open Disagreements between Al-Qaeda and Would-be Affiliates

Some debates over divisions between nationalist or liberation movements and al-Qaeda broadcast on the internet. And some local press have picked up on these stories. But it is not nearly enough exposure. Such stories, if identified, translated, and widely disseminated have the potential to raise doubts in the minds of Muslims worldwide.

Libyan Islamic Fighting Group members, for example, have held publicized reservations about forfeiting nationalist goals for al-Qaeda's international aspirations and giving up current tactics for a strategy of targeting civilians. Members openly deride al-Qaeda tactics as inherently flawed and unreligious.

Also, Abu Ja'afar Muhammad's (a well-known Algerian militant leader) tirade against al-Qaeda violence made local headlines. Such a statement from an anti-government leader known for his devotion to Islam and ferocity will play well to Muslim communities. In this case, even an active militant commander disavows al-Qaeda. But these examples must be brought to international awareness.

is anyone else doing this?

There is currently no effective counter-ideology campaign against al-Qaeda. Although foreign governments, independent groups, and individuals attempt modest and localized counter-marketing, there is little global effect thus far. This is clearly evidenced during online searches which yield infinitesimal counter-violence messages in a few languages compared with al-Qaeda's robust, reinforced, and redundant network of easily accessible online narratives and films in multiple languages and on numerous media platforms. Saudi Arabia, Indonesia, and several other countries' governments conduct some online messaging—but only in their languages targeting their citizens. And government affiliation undermines message impact.

Governments primarily focus on stopping specific attacks. Police and military operations to arrest and kill al-Qaeda operators and supporters are measurable and allow government leaders small and strategically meaningless victories.

But Al-Qaeda leadership, operators, financing, and supplies are regenerative and not strategic vulnerabilities.

So far al-Qaeda's message of violence to defend Islam against the West has outlasted leadership deaths and detainments. Al-Qaeda's message survives U.S. law enforcement and military victories. Al-Qaeda leaders are openly aware of their mortality and therefore put great stock into ensuring their messages sway new generations. The centrality of their messaging is evidenced by al-Qaeda's continued emphasis, effort, and money put into propaganda.

A few U.S. private citizens attempt to shut down websites. However, this effort is ineffective, as I explained. It takes minutes for a website creator to bring the site back up under a foreign and/or anonymous host. Instead, one must attack the validity of a webhost.

measuring success

The following are calculable measurements that could be used to see how identified, translated, and disseminated messages resound and reverberate in Muslim communities:

- Numbers of views of websites with anti-violence messages.

- Number of online news and blog sources referencing or copying identified, translated, and disseminated messages.

- Time al-Qaeda leadership spend on taped and videoed messages defending against criticism compared to past.

- Changes in polls of global support for al-Qaeda and affiliates.

- Major media network (CNN, FOX, MSNBC, Al Jazeera, Al Arabiyya) time spent on counter-messages.

- Number of opinion articles in major publications (*Sharq al Awsat, Al Hayat, Al Quds*) using arguments against al-Qaeda compared with the past.

so what does this mean for you?

You can do this! Yes you. You can create a website for almost no money and post counter-violence messages. The more sites the better. Al-Qaeda and thousands of independent supporters are doing just this. So you should too. You can help completely drown out sites supporting al-Qaeda. That way, when any curious young person wants to learn about how to fight perceived injustices they will see that killing for al-Qaeda is heresy and a lost cause. With a group of others or alone, anyone can follow the simple model to identify, translate, and disseminate counter-violence messages from credentialed sources.

The structure of such a group (or the work flow for an individual) would be simple:

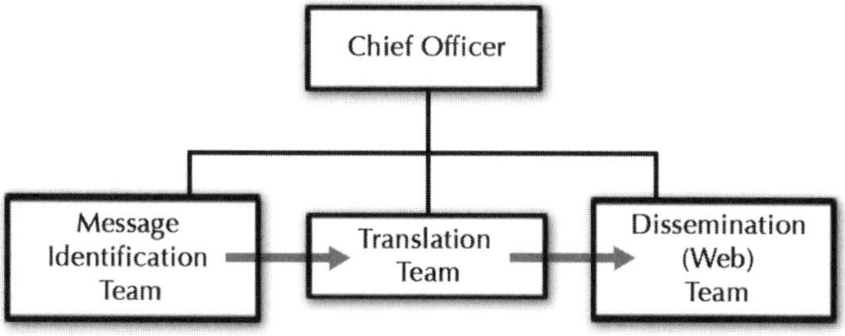

To test this out, I went to http://smallbusiness.yahoo.com /webhosting and signed up for a website ($8.96 per month for your first three months, $11.95 per month after). I downloaded Yahoo! sitebuilder for free at http://webhosting. yahoo.com and set up seventhpillar.net. In 37 minutes, I had five pages on the site with English quotes from four already translated anti-violence voices. And my training is in killing insurgents, not web design. If I can do it, anyone can do it. Here are some other sites where you can easily set up a web page of your own:

homestead.com
psyphire.com
esitesbuilder.com
web.com
wordpress.com
(This last is a terrorist favorite for creating easy blogs.)
...and a quick search will turn up many more too.

A non-profit organization might look like the following:

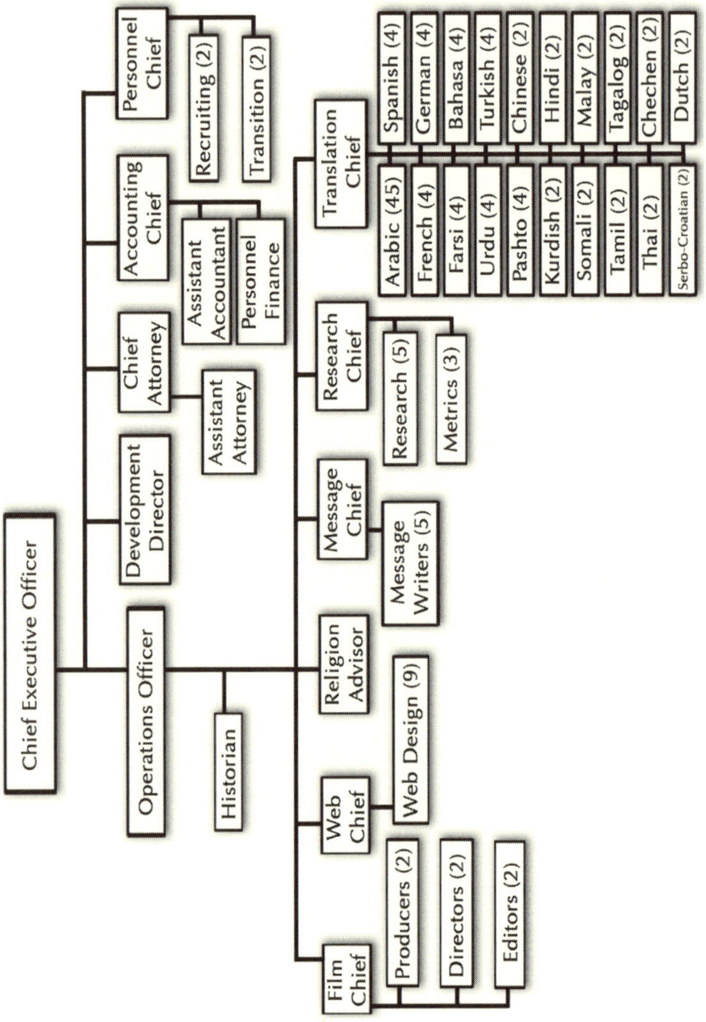
Chief Executive Officer
Operations Officer
Development Director
Chief Attorney
Assistant Attorney
Accounting Chief
Assistant Accountant
Personnel Finance
Personnel Chief
Recruiting (2)
Transition (2)
Historian
Film Chief
Producers (2)
Directors (2)
Editors (2)
Web Chief
Web Design (9)
Religion Advisor
Message Chief
Message Writers (5)
Research Chief
Research (5)
Metrics (3)
Translation Chief
Arabic (45)
French (4)
Farsi (4)
Urdu (4)
Pashto (4)
Kurdish (2)
Somali (2)
Tamil (2)
Thai (2)
Serbo-Croatian (2)
Spanish (4)
German (4)
Bahasa (4)
Turkish (4)
Chinese (2)
Hindi (2)
Malay (2)
Tagalog (2)
Chechen (2)
Dutch (2)

Chief Executive Officer

- Responsible for all operations and personnel.

Operations Officer

- Directs and is responsible for the identification, translation, and dissemination of counter-violence messages.

Historian

- Writes book on operations, successes, and failures for future generations who may face similar threats of extremism.

- Writes book on organization for large distribution and sale to credit all officers for their efforts.

- Conducts interviews of all employees as original sources for future historians and researchers.

Attorneys

- Advise Operations and Executive Officers on legality of all operations.

Hiring Officers

- Solicit applications for linguists.

- Schedule and conduct interviews to determine ability and suitability.

Transition Officers

- Responsible for relocation of new employees and their families.

Accounting Officers

- Appropriate money for IT support, web designers, translation tools, and administrative items as needed.

- Report to Executive Officer expected future needs.

Personnel Finance Officers

- Responsible for employee salaries, benefits, and transition costs.

- Report to Executive Officer expected future needs.

Film Producers, Directors, and Editors

- Continuously create films from already available media and online material to generate emotional responses.

- Continuously improve films for re-posting by web designers.

Web Designers

- Create, continuously improve, secure, and maintain a set of anonymous websites and mirror/sister sites using anonymous servers.

Linguists

- In the long run, an in-house translation team may simply be less expensive than outsourcing translations.
- Translate/interpret from English to other languages and vice versa.
- Edit/quality control translations.

Message Writers

- Determine quotes, book sections, and article excerpts from independent counter-extremist messages to further disseminate.
- Draft statements of legitimacy and independence of messengers.

Researchers

- Find and recommend potentially influential counter-extremism messages in Arab press, Muslim media, online commentary, extremist retractions, and popular media.

Metrics Researchers

- Measure success of counter-violence messages that the organization issues:
  - Numbers of views of websites with anti-violence messages.

- Number of online news and blog sources referencing or copying identified, translated, and disseminated messages.

- Time al-Qaeda leadership spend on taped and videoed messages defending against criticism compared to past.

- Changes in polls of global support for al-Qaeda and affiliates.

- Major media network (CNN, FOX, MSNBC, Al Jazeera, Al Arabiyya) time spent on counter-messages.

- Number of opinion articles in major publications (*Sharq al Awsat, Al Hayat, Al Quds*) using arguments against al-Qaeda compared with the past.

o Advise Chief Executive Officer on changes and recommend mission adjustments.

<u>Religion Advisor</u>

o Because of his study of and familiarity with Islamic texts, he can check the veracity and potential effectiveness of messages that the organization may identify for translation and dissemination.

o Trains employees to better identify potential messages that have religious weight.

- Advises Chief Executive Officer, Linguists, Researchers, and Message Writers.

conclusion

Driven to defend Islam against the West with romantic dreams of a heroic, David and Goliath-like fight that will end in paradise, al-Qaeda's followers will continue to grow as it stands now. However, effective counter-messaging will drive a permanent schism between mainstream Muslims and al-Qaeda. Although experts in intelligence, security, and academia agree on the centrality of winning the war of ideas, there is currently no concerted information plan to slow the spread of violent ideology. A determined counter-messaging effort must start immediately. Otherwise Americans will continue to spend untold sums and lives fighting these terrorists one at a time for centuries to come.

The fire that currently drives young Muslims to fight and die should be turned against al-Qaeda. Once radical leaders are ideologically isolated, recruitment pools will diminish. The active and passive support of Muslims, on which al-Qaeda and its affiliates rely, will die.

The war against al-Qaeda is a war for the hearts and minds of Muslims. It is a struggle within Islam. A strategy to identify, translate, and disseminate persuasive counter-al-Qaeda messages will end this struggle by completely turning Muslims against al-Qaeda.

notes & bibliography

Citations

Suicide bombers seek death specifically because at least part of Muslim societies venerates the sacrifice.—Robert Pape, *Dying to Win: The Strategic Logic of Suicide Terrorism*, Random House, 2006.

A 2006 Gallup World Poll of over 9,000 interviews in nine predominantly-Muslim countries found that radical Muslims are more likely to be wealthy and to have stayed in school longer than moderates.—Pew Research Center, Global Opinion Trends 2002-2007: A Rising Tide Lifts Mood in the Developing World, 2007.

A 2004 study of 132 terrorists, over 60% had some college education and 4% had a doctoral degree making this sample pool more educated than most in the third world.—Marc Sageman, *Understanding Terror Networks*, University of Pennsylvania Press, 2004.

A 2006 study of 242 European violent extremists concluded that socioeconomic background and criminal history of terrorists are similar to backgrounds of most young persons in immigrant Muslim communities in Europe.—Dr. Edwin Bakker, *Jihadi Terrorists in Europe*, Netherlands Institute of International Relations, 2006.

In a sample of 232 Arab suicide attackers associated with Lebananese and Palestinian groups and al-Qaeda from 1980-2003, they found that suicide bombers had similar education levels and socioeconomic status to the Palestinian and Lebanese publics.—Robert Pape, *Dying to Win: The Strategic Logic of Suicide Terrorism*, Random House, 2006.

Recent interviews with Palestinian suicide bomber dispatchers and failed suicide attackers, concluded that many terrorists did not have financial difficulties. Failed attackers held a standard of living comparable with most Palestinians.—Anat Berkom, *The Path to Paradise: The Inner World of Suicide Bombers and Their Dispatchers*, 2007

Recent evidence also supports the dissociation of extremism and wealth: the failed June 2007 U.K. airport attackers were well educated. All suspects were medical doctors but one who was an engineer with a PhD.—BBC, "Doctor Guilty of Car Bomb Attacks," http://news.bbc.co.uk/2/hi/uk_news/7773410.stm, 16 December 2008.

Modern extremism's "godfather" Sayyid Qutb's education exchange in the United States led him to despise what he perceived as the West's immorality. His observations while a student in the United States sparked his journey into radicalism after he returned home to Egypt—John L. Esposito, *Unholy War: Terror in the Name of Islam*, Oxford University Press, 2002.

Today, majorities in Bangledesh (93%), Morocco (92%), Indonesia (85%), Malaysia (81%), Turkey (77%), Palestinian Territory (73%), Pakistan (73%), Jordan (67%), Egypt (65%), Lebanon (64%) and Kuwait (63%) are "very" or "somewhat" worried that the United States could become a military threat.—Pew Research Center, *Global Opinion Trends 2002-2007: A Rising Tide Lifts Mood in the Developing World*, 2007.

Violence in the name of Islam has even become a fad in some Muslim countries. "Jihadi cool," distrust of the United States, and hatred for U.S. "humiliation" of Muslims have permeated Muslim communities worldwide.—Jessica Stern, *Jihad: A Global Fad*, Boston Globe, 1 August 2006.

Currently, the Internet is the primary media on which al-Qaeda markets their messages.—Sharon Cardash, Frank Cillufo, Jan Lane, Gregory Saathoff, Andrew Whitehead, "Networked Radicalization: A Counter-Strategy," The George Washington University Homeland Security Policy Institute & The University of Virginia Critical Analysis Group, 2006.

Currently, al-Qaeda's robust, reinforced and redundant network of easily accessible online narratives and films in multiple languages and on numerous media platforms is unchallenged. Al-Qaeda pours money, time and manpower into their online empire.—Dr. Bruce Hoffman, "The Use of the Internet by Islamic Extremists," Statement before the U.S. House of Representatives Permanent Select Committee on Intelligence, 4 May 2006. National Coordinator for Counterterrorism, "Jihadis and the Internet," Netherlands Ministries of Justice and of the Interior and Kingdom Relations, http://english.nctb.nl/Images/Jihadis %20and%20the%20Internet_tcm127-139397.pdf, February 2007. Craig Whitlock, "Al-Qaeda's Growing Online Offensive," Washington Post, http://www.washingtonpost.com/wpdyn/content/article/2008/06/23/AR2008062 30213_pf.html, 24 June 2008.

A publicized U.K. study, based on hundreds of incarcerated terrorists and terrorist associates, concludes that effective online messaging is crucial to radicalization.—Alan Travis, "The Making of an Extremist," Guardian.co.uk, 20 August 2008.

A Homeland Security Policy Institute study of eight major terrorism cases—to include the 2004 Madrid bombers and 2005 London bombers—concludes that online messaging was critical to radicalization.—Sharon Cardash, Frank Cillufo, Jan Lane, Gregory Saathoff, Andrew Whitehead, "Networked Radicalization: A Counter-Strategy," The George Washington University Homeland Security Policy Institute & The University of Virginia Critical Analysis Group, 2006.

Internet messages directly radicalized the convicted planners of the 2006 Fort Dix New Jersey plot to kill U.S. soldiers, according to court documents.—United States District Court, District of New Jersey, United States of America versus Mohamad Ibrahim Shnewer, Dritan Duka, Eljkir Duka, Shain Duka, and Serdar Tatar, Government Exhibit Ciminal Number 07-459, (conversation: 23 February 2007, 7:31 pm). United States District Court, District of New Jersey, United States of America versus Mohamad Ibrahim Shnewer, Dritan Duka, Eljkir Duka, Shain Duka, and Serdar Tatar, Government Exhibit Ciminal Number 07-459, (conversation: 23 February 2007, 9:39 pm)

Just one of many examples of professional, easily searchable, radicalizing message streams is the "Jihad Press." Found in English and Arabic online searches, the professional-looking and extremely-well-written Arabic online newspaper advocates al-Qaeda violence as an answer to everyday Muslim concerns over Western imposition in the Islamic World.—International Institute for Counter-Terrorism, "Calls for Carrying out Terrorist Attacks against Danish Targets," November 2008.

From his new home in Yemen, New Mexico-born Anwar Nassar al-Awlaki publishes written and audio lectures commanding Muslims all over the world to attack the United States and its interests at all times under any and all circumstances. His lecture "Constants on the Path of Jihad," for example, persuades Muslims towards violence in no uncertain terms and is available widely on the internet. In simple, straight-forward American vernacular, the lecture is available on hundreds of independent websites.

—Anwar al-Alawki, Constants of Jihad, http://www.scribd.com/doc/2407141/Constants-on-the-Path-of-Jihad, 2006.

Anwar al-Awlaki posted "44 Ways of Supporting Jihad" on January 5, 2009 on his website. The essay commands every Muslim to focus every resource and effort towards violence against Western and secular governments and details how Muslims can help al-Qaeda marketing. Awlaki explains to readers how to identify, translate, and disseminate violent teachings and commands in support of al-Qaeda. Within only 24 hours, this essay received over 1,000 downloads. And within 24 hours, 61 other websites reposted the paper.—http://www.anwar-alawlaki.com/, accessed 10 January 2009.

Another example of an extremist website easily found online was inshallahshahedd.muslimpar.com in October 2007. This site, run by an American Muslim in North Carolina, offered up translations and soundbites of messages encouraging violent attacks against Americans.—Michael Moss, "An Internet Jihad Aims at U.S. Viewers," New York Times, http://www.nytimes.com/2007/10/15/us/15net.html?_r=2&ref=world, 15 October 2007. Marc Lynch, *Al-Qaeda's Media Strategies*, The National Interest Online, http://www.nationalinterest.org.aspx?id=11524, 1 March 2006.

The importance of translation is highlighted in the radicalization of Mohammad Sidique Khan, mastermind of the July 7, 2005 attacks on London's subway. According to his brother, Khan could not relate to the local non-violent imam because of the language barrier. Khan spoke English. The imam taught only in Urdu and Arabic.—Shiv Malik, My Brother the Bomber, Prospect,
http://www.prospect-magazine.co.uk/article_details.php?id =9635, June 2007.

His renunciation of al-Qaeda's terrorist tactics confronts killing over ethnicity, use of human shields, and destruction of non-Muslim property.—Lawrence Wright, "The Rebellion Within: An Al Qaeda Mastermind Questions Terrorism," The New Yorker http://www.newyorker.com/reporting/2008/06/02/080602fa_fact_wright, 2 June 2008.

His "Foundations of the Preparation for Jihad" is the book al-Qaeda uses to justify violent jihadists actions and establish its group structure worldwide.—Combating Terrorism Center, West Point, *The Militant Ideology Atlas Executive Report*, November 2006.

Sayyid Imam's critics claim that the Egyptian government tortured and forced the recantation. His detractors even maintain that Sayyid Imam is a pawn of the West.—Peter Bergen and Paul Cruickshank, "The Unraveling: The Jihadist Revolt against bin Laden," The New Republic http://www.tnr.com/politics/story.html?id=702bf6d5-a37a-4e3e-a491-fd72bf6a9da1, 11 June 2008.

Zawahiri wrote a 188-page defense against the book.—Exoneration: A Treatise Exonerating the Community of the Pen and the Sword from the Debilitating Accusation of Fatigue and Weakness, Ekhlas web forum,
http://www.ek-ls.org/forum/showthread.php?t=127920&highlight=%C3%ED%E3%E4, 2008

Other reformed extremist messages also have the potential to undermine al-Qaeda's ideology, such as bin Ladin's former mentor Salman al-Awdah's 2007 editorial attack on bin Ladin...—Shaykh Salman al-Awdah, "A Ramadan Letter to Osama bin Laden," http://muslimmatters.org/2007/09/18/shaykh-salman-al-oudahs-ramadan-letter-to-osama-bin-Laden-on-nbc/, 2007.

...former terrorist leader of Southeast Asia Jamaah Islamiyah Nasir Abas' interviews and book Exposing Jamaah Islamiyah criticizing al-Qaeda-style violence...—Scott Atran, "To Jihad and Back," (Book review of Nasir Abas' Unveiling Jamaah Islamiyah: Confessions

of an Ex- JI Member) Foreign Policy, http://www.foreignpolicy.com/users/login.php?story_id=3279&URL=http://www.foreign policy. com/story/ cms.php?story_id=3279, November/December 2005.

...rehabilitated imprisoned Saudi extremist renunciations.—Jason Burke, "Saudis Offer Pioneering Therapy for Ex-Jihadists," The Observer, http://www.guardian.co.uk/world/ 2008/mar/09/saudiarabia.terrorism, 9 March 2008.

Several governments including Saudi Arabia and Indonesia have used the term to describe Islamic terrorists publicly, and al-Qaeda has spent time and money to defend against the accusation.—Ayman al-Zawahiri, Audio/Video/Written Statements and interviews from 1999 – today, http://www1.nefafoundation.org:80/documents-aqstatements.html. Usama bin Ladin, Audio/Video/Written Statements and interviews from 1999 – today, http://www1.nefafoundation.org:80/documents-aqstatements.html.

One example is the potentially tide-shifting February 2008 Deobandi fatwa of 6,000 members in India against violence in the name of religion, publically reconfirmed by the members in October 2008. The conservative Muslim Deobandi-sect leadership and ideals have influenced the Taliban, and the movement's ideologues appear independent from government influence.—Grand Mufti Habibur Rehman, "Fatwa Against Terrorism" (in English), Darul Uloom Deoband http://madrasareforms.blogspot.com/2008/06/text-of-darul-uloom-deobands-fatwa.html, February 2008

For Kharijites, the ends justified the means. Violence was not just allowed. It was compulsory.—John L. Esposito, *Unholy War: Terror in the Name of Islam*, Oxford University Press, 2002.

As one of al-Qaeda's forefathers, Muhammad al-Faraj, wrote in his influential book The Neglected Duty: "There is no doubt that the idols of this world can only disappear through the power of the sword.—Muhammad 'Abd al-Salam Faraj, *Al-Faridah al-Gha'ibah*, translated by Johanne J. G. Jansen, MacMillan Publishing Company, New York, 1986.

In a September 2007 statement, top al-Qaeda lieutenant Abu Yahya al-Libi even admitted that comparisons to the Qaramita would injure al-Qaeda credibility in the eyes of mainstream Muslims.—Jarret Brachman, Abu Yahya's Six Easy Steps for Defeating al-Qaeda, Perspectives on Terrorism, Volume I Issue 5, http://www.terrorismanalysts.com /pt/index.php?option=com_rokzine&view=article&id=18&Itemid=54, 2007.

Of the modern authors, Sayyid Qutb (executed by the Egyptian government in 1966) has the greatest influence.—Combating Terrorism Center, West Point, *The Militant Ideology Atlas Executive Report*, November 2006.

Usama Bin Ladin, himself, is one of the top thirteen most influential modern militant authors.—Combating Terrorism Center, West Point, *The Militant Ideology Atlas Executive Report*, November, 2006.

Dubbing al-Qaeda followers as..."qutbists,"...—because they openly praise these ideologues such as Sayyid Qutb.—Combating Terrorism Center, West Point, *The Militant Ideology Atlas Executive Report*, November 2006.

An extensive study found support for terrorist tactics has declined in seven out of eight countries...—Pew Research Center, *Global Opinion Trends 2002-2007: A Rising Tide Lifts Mood in the Developing World*, 2007.

Few...want to support a lost cause.—David C. Rapoport, *The Four Waves of Modern Terrorism*, http://www.isop.ucla.edu/article.asp?parentid=47153, 5 June 2006.

Foreign and Iraqi fighters willingly remained in Fallujah, Iraq in November 2004....

the border with Syria, holed up in the basements of houses to die fighting Americans in July 2005.—Interviews.

Al-Qaeda's narrative stresses that the movement will continue long after the leaders' deaths. Bin Ladin and all his deputies are openly aware of their mortality and also need their followers to die.—Usama bin Ladin, Audio/Video/Written Statements and interviews from 1999 – today, http://www1.nefafoundation.org:80/documents-aqstatements.html.

Al-Qaeda relies on the image of integrity at the top echelon of its marketing pyramid: "As Sahab," "Al Fajr" and the "Global Islamic Media Front" marketing networks.—Marc Lynch, *Al-Qaeda's Media Strategies*, The National Interest Online, http://www.nationalinterest.org.aspx?id=11524, 1 March 2006.

A recent media rumor of Saudi government infiltration shut down and ratcheted up security for the entire Global Islamic Media Front (hundreds of websites) temporarily.—Christopher Boucek, *Fears of Intelligence Penetration of the GIMF*, Jamestown, Volume 3, Issue 16, http://www.jamestown.org/terrorism/news/article.php?articleid=2369974, 25 April 2006.

Libyan Islamic Fighting Group members, for example, have held publicized reservations about forfeiting nationalist goals for al-Qaeda's international aspirations and giving up current tactics for a strategy of targeting civilians. Members openly deride al-Qaeda tactics as inherently flawed and unreligious.—Peter Bergen and Paul Cruickshank, "The Unraveling: The Jihadist Revolt against bin Laden," The New Republic http://www.tnr.com/politics/story.html?id=702bf6d5-a37a-4e3e-a491-fd72bf6a9da1, 11 June 2008.

Also, Abu Ja'afar Muhammad's (a well-known Algerian militant leader) tirade against Al-Qaeda violence made local headlines. Such a statement from an anti-government leader known for his devotion to Islam and ferocity will play well to Muslim communities.—Muhammad Abu Jaafar,"Salafist Protectors against Bombings Afflicting Muslims in Algeria," http://dhdsdz.blogspot.com/2008/01/blog-post_3547.html, 2008.

Saudi Arabia, Indonesia and several other countries' governments conduct some online messaging—but only in their local languages targeting their citizens.—The Jakarta Post, *Former Jihad Members Get Lecture*, 16 January 2006. Christopher Boucek, *Extremism Reeducation and Rehabilitation in Saudi Arabia*, Terrorism Monitor, The Jamestown Foundation, Volume V, Issue 16, 16 August 2007.

Primary Sources

Abas, Nasir, *Membongkar Jamaah Islamiyah: Pengakuan Mantan Anggota JI* (Unveiling Jamaah Islamiyah: Confessions of an Ex- JI Member), Jakarta: Grafindo Khazanah Ilmu, 2005.

al-Awdah, Salman, "Positive Alternatives," http://www.islamtoday.com/showme_weekly_2006.cfm?cat_id=30&sub_cat_id=1659, 2006.

al-Awdah, Salman, "A Ramadan Letter to Osama bin Laden," http://muslimmatters.org/2007/09/18/shaykh-salman-al-oudahs-ramadan-letter-to-osama-bin-laden-on-nbc/, 2007.

al-Awdah, Salman, "We Must be Unequivocal in Condemning Violence," http://www.islamtoday.com/showme_weekly_2006.cfm?cat_id=30&sub_cat_id=1134, 2006.

al-Awlaki, Anwar, "Constants of Jihad," http://www.scribd.com/doc/2407141/Constants-on-the-Path-of-Jihad, 2006.

Center for Moderate Muslim Indonesia on Radio Republic Indonesia, Interview with Nasir Abas, http://www.indonesiamatters.com/104/nasir-abas-on-jamaah-islamiyah/, February 2006.

Faraj, Muhammad 'Abd al-Salam, *Al-Faridah al-Gha'ibah (The Neglected Duty)*, translated by Johanned J. G. Jansen, MacMillan Publishing Company, New York, 1986.

Jaafar, Muhammad Abu,"Salafist Protectors against Bombings Afflicting Muslims in Algeria," http://dhdsdz.blogspot.com/2008/01/blog-post_3547.html, 2008.

Ladin, Usama bin, Audio/Video/Written Statements and interviews from 1999 – today, http://www1.nefafoundation.org:80/documents-aqstatements.html.

Qutb, Sayyid, *Ma'alim fi-l-Tariq (Milestones)*, Dar al-Ilm, Damascus, Syria.

Rehman, Grand Mufti Habibur, "Fatwa Against Terrorism" (in English), Darul Uloom Deoband http://madrasareforms.blogspot.com/2008/06/text-of-darul-uloom-deobands-fatwa.html, February 2008.

al-Sharif, Sayyid Imam, *Exposure of the Exoneration Book* (in 13 episodes), Al-Misri Al-Yawm daily newspaper, November-December 2008.

al-Sharif, Sayyid Imam, *Foundations for the Preparation of Jihad*, 1988.

al-Sharif, Sayyid Imam, *Wathiqat Tarshid Al-'Aml Al-Jihadi fi Misr w'Al-'Alam (Advice Regarding the Conduct of Jihadist Action in Egypt and the World)*, Aljareeda.com in chapters, 19 November 2007 – 5 December 2007.

al-Zawahiri, Ayman, Audio/Video/Written Statements and interviews from 1999 – today, http://www1.nefafoundation.org:80/documents-aqstatements.html.

al-Zawahiri, Ayman, *The Exoneration: A Treatise Exonerating the Community of the Pen and the Sword from the Debilitating Accusation of Fatigue and Weakness*, Ekhlas web forum,
http://www.ek-ls.org/forum/showthread.php?t=127920&highlight=%C3%ED%E3%E4, 2008.

al-Zawahiri, Ayman, "Knights Under the Prophet's Banner," Serialized in Al-Sharq al-Awsat (London, December 2, 2001) from Marc Sageman's *Understanding Terror Networks*, University of Pennsylvania Press, 2004.

al-Zayyat, Montasser, *The Road to al-Qaeda: the Story of Bin Laden's Right-Hand Man*, translated by Ahmed Fekry, Pluto Press, Sterling, Virginia, 2004.

Surveys & Polls (and Studies Comprising Surveys & Polls)

Bakker, Dr. Edwin, *Jihadi Terrorists in Europe*, Netherlands Institute of International Relations, 2006.

Berko, Anat, *The Path to Paradise: The Inner World of Suicide Bombers and Their Dispatchers*, Praeger Security International, 2007.

Cardash, Sharon; Cillufo, Frank; Lane, Jan; Saathoff, Gregory; Whitehead, Andrew, "Networked Radicalization: A Counter-Strategy," The George Washington University Homeland Security Policy Institute & the University of Virginia Critical Analysis Group, 2006.

Combating Terrorism Center, West Point, *The Militant Ideology Atlas Executive Report*,

November, 2006.

Pape, Robert, *Dying to Win: The Strategic Logic of Suicide Terrorism*, Random House, 2006.

Pew Research Center, *Global Opinion Trends 2002-2007: A Rising Tide Lifts Mood in the Developing World*, http://pewglobal.org/reports/display.php?ReportID=257, 2007.

Sageman, Marc, *Understanding Terror Networks*, University of Pennsylvania Press, 2004.

United Nations Assistance Mission to Afghanistan, *Suicide Attacks in Afghanistan (2001-2007)*, 2007.

Articles and Books on al-Qaeda Strategy, Narrative, and Counter-Voices

Asharq Al-Awsat website, "Jailed al-Qa'ida Ideologue Urges Halt to Attacks Contradicting Islamic Law," 8 May 2007.

Atran, Scott, "To Jihad and Back," (Book review of Nasir Abas' Unveiling Jamaah Islamiyah: Confessions of an Ex- JI Member) Foreign Policy, http://www.foreignpolicy.com/users/login.php?story_id=3279&URL=http://www.foreign policy.com/story/cms.php?story_id=3279, November/December 2005.

BBC, "Doctor Guilty of Car Bomb Attacks," http://news.bbc.co.uk/2/hi/uk_news/7773410.stm, 16 December 2008.

Bergen, Peter; Cruickshank, Paul, "The Unraveling: The Jihadist Revolt against bin Laden," The New Republic (http://www.tnr.com/politics/story.html?id=702bf6d5-a37a-4e3e-a491-fd72bf6a9da1), 11 June 2008.

Black, Andrew, *The Ideological Struggle Over al-Qaeda's Suicide Tactics in Algeria*, Terrorism Monitor Volume 6, Issue 3, 7 February 2008.

Black, Ian, "Revisionist Message From Pioneer of Violent Jihad Shakes Al-Qa'ida," The Guardian Weekly, 3 August 2007.

Blakely, Rhys, "Darool-Uloom Deoband Issues Fatwa against Terrorism," Times Online, http://www.timesonline.co.uk/tol/news/world/asia/article4045862.ece, 2 June 2008.

Boucek, Christopher, "Extremism Reeducation and Rehabilitation in Saudi Arabia," Terrorism Monitor, The Jamestown Foundation, Volume V, Issue 16, 16 August 2007.

Brachman, Jarret, "Abu Yahya's Six Easy Steps for Defeating al-Qaeda," Perspectives on Terrorism, Volume I Issue 5, http://www.terrorismanalysts.com/pt/index.php?option=com_rokzine&view=article&id=18&Itemid=54, 2007.

The Brookings Institute, *Iraq Index: Tracking Variables of Reconstruction & Security in Post-Saddam Iraq*, http://www.brookings.edu/fp/saban/iraq/index.pdf, 16 August 2007.

Burke, Jason, "Saudis Offer Pioneering Therapy for Ex-Jihadists," The Observer, http://www.guardian.co.uk/world/2008/mar/09/saudiarabia.terrorism, 9 March 2008.

Cleveland, William, *A History of the Modern Middle East*, Westview Press, Oxford, 1994.

Cruickshank, Paul, "How Muslim extremists are turning on Osama Bin Laden," New York Daily News, http://www.nydailynews.com/opinions/2008/06/08/2008-06-08_how_muslim_extremists_are_turning_on_osa.html, 8 June 2008.

Esposito, John L., *Unholy War: Terror in the Name of Islam*, Oxford University Press, 2002.

Kepel, Gilles, *Jihad: The Trail of Political Islam*, translated by Anthony F. Roberts, Harvard University Press, Cambridge, 2002.

Kepel, Gilles, *Muslim Extremism in Egypt: The Prophet and Pharaoh*, translated by Jon Rothschild, University of California Press, 2003.

Haddad, Yvonne Y., "Sayyid Qutb: Ideologue of Islamic Revival," in John L. Esposito (ed.), Voices of Resurgent Islam, Oxford University Press, 1983.

Hoffman, Dr. Bruce, "The Use of the Internet by Islamic Extremists," Statement before the U.S. House of Representatives Permanent Select Committee on Intelligence, 4 May 2006.

International Institute for Counter-Terrorism, "Calls for Carrying out Terrorist Attacks against Danish Targets," November 2008.

International Research Center, "Zawahiri Tries to Clear Name, Explain Strategy," http://www.fas.org/irp/eprint/zawahiri.pdf, April 2008.

The Jakarta Post, "Former Jihad Members Get Lecture," 16 January 2006.

Lynch, Marc, "Al-Qaeda's Media Strategies," The National Interest Online, http://www.nationalinterest.org.aspx?id=11524, 1 March 2006.

Malik, Shiv, "My Brother the Bomber," Prospect, http://www.prospect-magazine.co.uk/article_details.php?id=9635, June 2007.

Moss, Michael, "An Internet Jihad Aims at U.S. Viewers," New York Times, http://www.nytimes.com/2007/10/15/us/15net.html?_r=2&ref=world, 15 October 2007.

National Coordinator for Counterterrorism, "Jihadis and the Internet," Netherlands Ministries of Justice and of the Interior and Kingdom Relations, http://english.nctb.nl/Images/Jihadis%20and%20the%20Internet_tcm127-139397.pdf, February 2007.

Rapoport, David C., *The Four Waves of Modern Terrorism*, http://www.isop.ucla.edu/article.asp?parentid=47153, 5 June 2006.

Stern, Jessica, *Jihad: A Global Fad*, Boston Globe, 1 August 2006.

Travis, Alan, "The Making of an Extremist," guardian.co.uk, 20 August 2008.

Ulph, Stephen, "Fears of Intelligence Penetration of the GIMF," Jamestown, Volume 3, Issue 16, http://www.jamestown.org/terrorism/news/article.php?articleid=2369974, April 25, 2006.

United Press International, "Al Qaeda Tapes Grow in Number, Expertise," http://insider.washingtontimes.com/news/2007/sep/24/al-qaeda-tapes-grow32in-number-expertise/, 24 September 2007.

Whitlock, Craig, "Al-Qaeda's Growing Online Offensive," Washington Post, http://www.washingtonpost.com/wpdyn/content/article/2008/06/23/AR2008062302135_pf.html, 24 June 2008.

Wright, Lawrence, The Looming Tower: Al-Qaeda and the Road to 9/11, Random House Inc, 2006.

Wright, Lawrence, "My Trip to Al-Qaeda," Lecture, Washington, DC, 27 September 2007.

Wright, Lawrence, "The Rebellion Within: An Al Qaeda Mastermind Questions Terrorism," The New Yorker http://www.newyorker.com/reporting/2008/06/02/080602fa_fact_wright, 2 June 2008.

To order books with free shipping,
or for further notes, updates,
free content to disseminate,
special offers, or even just to say hi,
please visit

www.InThreeEasySteps.com